Praise for *I Want to B*

"'Your future story is yours, and you are the author.' Ashley captures the hearts of kids and adults alike as she shares a message of hope and empowerment. *I Want to Be a Lot* shares a necessary message that shatters the status quo of society and breaking the mold to find personal happiness. Through a personal narrative, Ashley invites kids, parents, and educators to reflect upon what each hopes for in order to find their place in society. This is a great gift for children and a great way to spark dialogue as they dream for their tomorrow."

—Roman Nowak, teacher and agent of transformation at É.S.C. L'Escale

"I love this book! Ashley truly hits the mark with her first book, *I Want to Be A Lot!* Who knows what they want when we are in school? Does it matter? The message and illustrations take us on a journey that shows us it is okay to change our minds! Cheers to a wonderful book that belongs in every school library and classroom!"

—Jeff Kubiak, educator, author of *One Drop of Kindness*, speaker and advocate for #AllKids

"I loved this sweet book. The idea of any of us having to be just 'one thing' is so antiquated. We can and should be helping students realize that their gifts, talents, and interests don't always fit into one box. They can be 'a lot' more than just one thing!"

—Todd Nesloney, educator, speaker, and coauthor of *Kids Deserve It!*

"Ashley Savage has composed a masterpiece for all ages! You will be moved by Willow's journey of self-discovery. As I read this book, I imagined reading this aloud to my three daughters when they were younger. This book is a perfect conversation starter between parents, educators, and kids on the limitless possibilities before us. I also envision this book as a wonderful way to engage educators on how to inspire our kids to change the world. Ashley Savage writes from the heart, and you will be inspired by her beautiful worlds along with the artistry of Genesis Kohler's illustrations. Adding this title to your bookshelf will fill your heart and encourage you to connect with kids on how they want to be a lot."

—Sean Gaillard, principal and author of *The Pepper Effect*

I Want to Be a Lot
©2019 by Ashley Savage

All rights reserved. No part of this publication may be reproduced in any form or by any electronic or mechanical means, including information storage and retrieval systems, without permission in writing by the publisher, except by a reviewer who may quote brief passages in a review. For information regarding permission, contact the publisher at books@daveburgessconsulting.com.

This book is available at special discounts when purchased in quantity for use as premiums, promotions, fundraisers, or for educational use. For inquiries and details, contact the publisher at books@daveburgessconsulting.com.

For more books from Dave Burgess Consulting, Inc., visit DaveBurgessConsulting.com/dbcibooks.

Published by Dave Burgess Consulting, Inc.
San Diego, CA
DaveBurgessConsulting.com

Cover Design and Illustrations by Genesis Kohler
Editing and Interior Design by My Writers' Connection

Paperback ISBN: 978-1-949595-43-7
Hardcover: 978-1-949595-45-1
LCCN: 2019941889

First Printing: June 2019

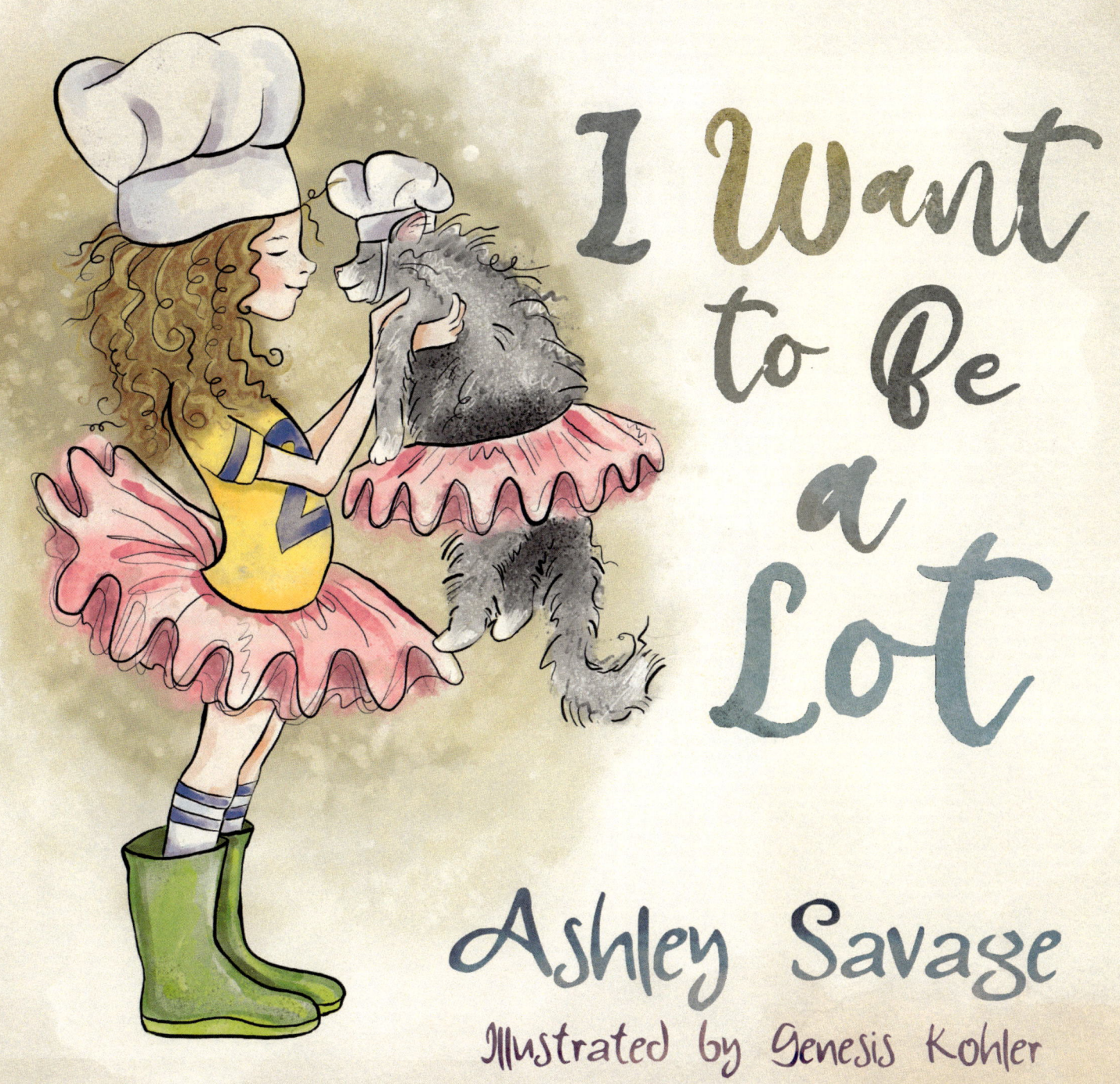

I Want to Be a Lot

Ashley Savage

Illustrated by Genesis Kohler

To the dreamers: I believe in you.

I believe in
your dreams,
and I believe
in your ability
to be a lot.

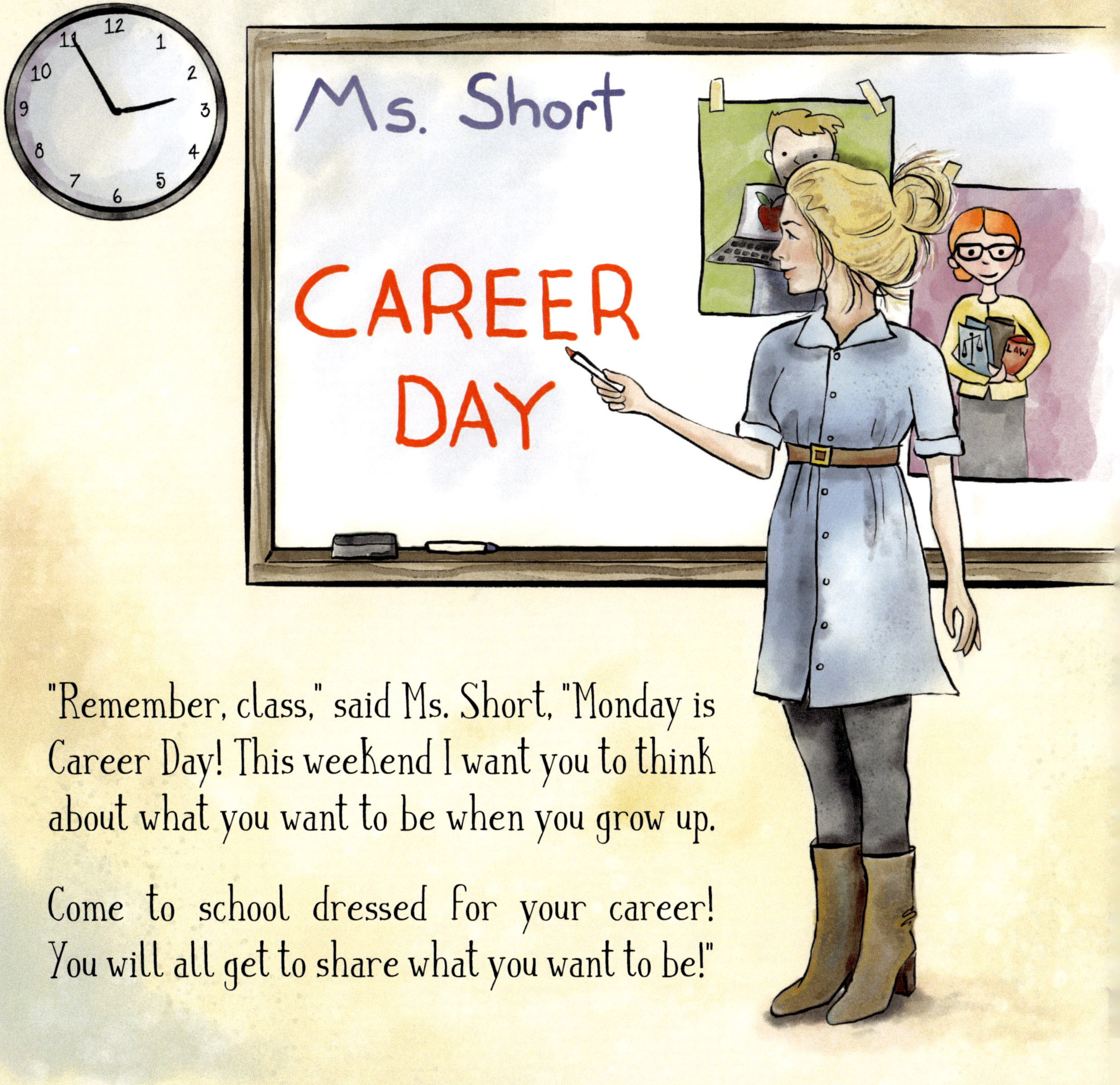

"Remember, class," said Ms. Short, "Monday is Career Day! This weekend I want you to think about what you want to be when you grow up.

Come to school dressed for your career! You will all get to share what you want to be!"

"Mom, did you always know what you wanted to be?" I asked.

"Not exactly. But I always knew what I loved to do, so that's where I started. Cooking was something I enjoyed, which led me to culinary school. After I became a chef, I used my love for writing to write a cookbook. I was able to do what I love and share it with the world through my writing."

"Hmmm... Maybe I'll be a chef for career day. I do love to cook with you."

"I can't pick just one thing! There are so many things I like to do."

"Don't worry, Willow," Mom said when she kissed me goodnight. "Get some rest, sweetie. You don't have to decide tonight. Maybe you and Gramps can talk about it more at lunch tomorrow."

"Gramps, have you always known what you wanted to be?"

"Y'know, kid, I didn't always know. I had a long career in the military, which I loved, but I had other interests too. Once I realized what I loved doing, I followed that. You don't have to do one thing forever, but you should do what you love."

"Thanks, Gramps. You always know what to say."

"I love art! There are no rules.

It's my ideas, my colors, my choices. There are no wrong answers. Maybe I should be an artist for career day."

"When I'm upset, my dad looks up crazy experiments for us to try. It helps me forget why I'm upset and remember how cool science is!

Maybe I should be a scientist for career day."

"My mom is always taking pictures—capturing small moments, like Dad and me napping on the couch, and big moments, like family vacations. I love taking pictures of nature, fun times with friends, and Mr. Einstein when he's sleeping."

"Dad, how can I pick just one thing to be?

I love cooking, science, taking pictures, painting, drawing, and so many other things!"

"Willow, it's okay to love a lot of things. You can love to make art and love to do science and love to take pictures. The important thing to remember is that you don't have to give up loving one to pursue the other. I have a great idea for how you can dress up for school on Monday."

"Today, I dressed up as a chef, an artist, a scientist, and a photographer because I love all those things. I don't want to be just one thing. I want to be a *lot*!"

"Ever since we were little, people have asked us, 'What do you want to be?' I never knew how to answer that question, so today I want to ask you a different question: 'What do you love? What makes you want to explore more?'

Maybe for you, it's math and science.

Maybe music is what calls you.

You don't have to be just one thing. Your future story is yours, and you are the author. Don't limit yourself. You can be anything."

"YOU can be A LOT."

Acknowledgments

To say this is a dream would be an understatement. There were so many people who were instrumental in this process. To the people who inspired me and the ones who made it all come true, here are my blessings:

Mom, thank you for being the lead driver and pushing me to work, create, and share my message. You've supported me in every hobby, career path, and job I've taken on, no matter how big or small. You knew what I was capable of before I even believed in myself, and I want to thank you for that. From encouraging my rough sketches of this book to reading through manuscript drafts to proofreading my emails, I genuinely couldn't have done this without you. You've been everything I've needed and more as my very own Momager.

Dad, thank you for telling me, even at my lowest, that you were proud of me. Every day you've shown me kindness, compassion, and support, and I can't even describe how thankful I am for you. We might call you Mom's fourth child because of how goofy you can be, but you're the best Dad anyone could ask for, and I'm proud to have you as mine. You both believed in me before anyone else did and it carried me throughout this process with confidence and inspiration.

Jacob, thank you for being unapologetically yourself at all times and reminding me to do the same. You've inspired me in every aspect of my life in more ways than you can imagine.

Haley, my little mini-me, thank you for being you. From dancing with me through the house to singing all the way to school, your company is never less than refreshing.

To my half-sister Emily (wink, wink): If I had one wish, it would be that the fun we experience every day wasn't through Facetime calls but rather in person. Wherever I go, you bring me home.

Ethan, your laughter keeps me sane. From spa resorts to our little living room, your company is my favorite. Thanks for being my favorite Savage.

Papaw, you are the man who taught me what it means to be generous of heart and kind in nature. You show me daily what it's like to live on mission. Out of all the things I want to be, I want to be most like you.

To the woman who taught me how to spread my ideas and messages in more than one way: Mimi, Thank you for being one of the kindest souls I know and teaching me what it means to rise above the challenges in life.

Aunt Lisa, you are my home away from home. From home-cooked meals to summer break, this time I am talking about you! Thank you for the endless laughter.

Aunt Heather, you are one of the hardest working women I know. Thank you for showing me that perseverance and dedication pays off. Our conversations have been some of my favorite moments in life.

To Dave and Shelley Burgess for taking a risk on a nineteen-year-old author: Not many publishers would do that. Your belief and support in student voice will forever be appreciated.

To the DBC, Inc. team for preparing, planning, and bringing *I Want to Be a Lot* to completion: I am so grateful to each one of you for the hard work you put into making this dream come true. Erin, Mariana, and Genesis, thank you for your patience and indulging me in the struggle to get my vision down on paper. You are all amazing, and I am so thankful for your guidance through this process.

I am so grateful to each person mentioned here and so many more who weren't mentioned. You have inspired me and supported me throughout my life and throughout this process. My hope is that *I Want to Be a Lot* will resonate with readers, and they, too, will feel inspired and supported. Life is full of experiences to be had, and each one should be explored. Everyone has multiple passions, so don't limit yourself; choose to be a lot!

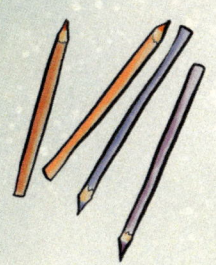

About the Author

Ashley Savage is a student at the University of Central Arkansas. She has experienced the pressure of trying to answer the age-old question, "What do you want to be?" While trying to think of how to respond, she had a revelation: She wanted to "be" a lot! Ashley is currently studying online journalism with a minor in creative writing. In her spare time, she enjoys practicing her photography and painting. She plans to pursue all the things she loves.

About the Illustrator

Genesis Kohler earned a BFA at the Herron School of Art in Indianapolis, Indiana. She lives in the west of Ireland with her husband and son and their cat, Faoiste (Fwee-shta, which means "fudge" in Irish). When she isn't creating art or reading, she tends to take way too many pictures of sheep.

Made in United States
Orlando, FL
28 November 2021